THE  EXPRESS

CARTOONS

FIFTY THIRD SERIES

GILES CHARACTERS™ & © 1999 Express Newspapers.
Published by

Pedigree®
BOOKS

The Old Rectory, Matford Lane, Exeter, Devon, EX2 4PS
Under licence from Express Newspapers.
Printed in Italy. ISBN 1-902836-12-X

£7.99

GI 53

An Introduction by

David Dimbleby

It is astonishing that Giles still has such appeal that each year we can welcome another Annual.
I was introduced to him by my father, who rated Giles his top cartoonist bar none, and used to regale
the family with an account of meeting his hero.

Every fan has his own reasons for liking Giles. For me it is not so much the events he comments on.
After all, elections and budgets, Motor shows or Smithfield shows, American servicemen and foreign
villains come and go. What lasts are the powerful characters. Their language and their lifestyle look a
little dated now but their essential characteristics are still those we find all around us. And the
draughtsmanship, as ever, is superb.

It would never do to admit it, but don't we all have in our family someone with just a trace,
just a hint, of the Giles family in them?

Happy browsing.

CONTENTS

Families

"Doesn't say a word about compensation for grievous bodily harm inflicted on a husband calling to collect his maintenance."

"Come home, Beatles - come back Precious Weed."

"Welcome to our Sunday Entertainments Department - Soames Forsyte kicks the bucket tonight."

"If there's one time I'd devolution the lot of 'em it's when Grandma's sister from Inveraray sings Scotland the Brave."

"Dead easy - stick a bone in the ground, he digs it up, I get the garden done, and Bruno gets his exercise."

"Dropping 'em all in a pool of Piranha fish is not what Lord Justice Lawton had in mind when he called for a return to discipline and traditional moral standards."

"No dear, Anna Ford's lucky - she can't see daddy at breakfast time."

"Grandma is playing 'Statue of Liberty' not 'Hitch-hiker's Guide to the Galaxy!' "

"Okay, Hurricane Higgins - Easter's over!"

"So much for parental control - they've been looting again."

"I'd gladly give up decorating the living room so Vera could have her new gold tooth."

"Now we know what to do with Grandma this weekend."

"I'm glad they didn't ask your Dad to do an alphabet - everything starting with a letter B."

Children

"This beats all your Father Christmases."

"O wretched boy!"

"Natives of Birmingham TO ARMS! And drive the invaders from our fair plains of Sutton Coldfield."

"Good afternoon, gentlemen - I believe we are of those who protest at having our fingerprints taken at school."

"Who said yesterday he'd like to see anybody get <u>him</u> on this Jumpology nonsense?"

" 'HEAD MASTER PREFERS TO BEAT BOYS WITH CRICKET BAT.' Yesterday's fascinating headline which had nothing to do with the Budget or the coming of General de Gaulle."

"If it's not all right for me to plug in my electric guitar for five minutes why is it all right for Grandma to sit reading in the bathroom all evening?"
(Power cuts due to striking power workers)

"With the absence of competition from Mrs. Sharples, Matt Dillon and Burke's Law, may I expect our homework to be at least partly legible?"
(Commercial TV goes on strike for seven days)

"They want to know if they can go fishing in your barn."

"Monday: Cricket - Scouts v. Sea Cadets, our house, lunch one o'clock. Tuesday: Baseball - our house, early buffet lunch, tea, four o'clock. Wednesday..."

Holiday/Travel

GRANDMA GILES'S PROGRESS: AN INTERIM REPORT...

GRANDMA GILES'S Blackpool holiday has been a strenuous business, and we feel that she and sister Millie should be given a day's rest. So should the readers. But a final monstrous holiday cartoon will appear from the North to-morrow.

GILES

"No fear! We'll toss for it. I served them when they were here last year."

"First time your Father's smiled this holiday - when they told him he'd got to rejoin his regiment for Kenya."

"No Madam, it's not pirates - it's the steward with your damned elevenses, and we've been in dock for two days."
(Spanish pirates seize liner Santa Maria)

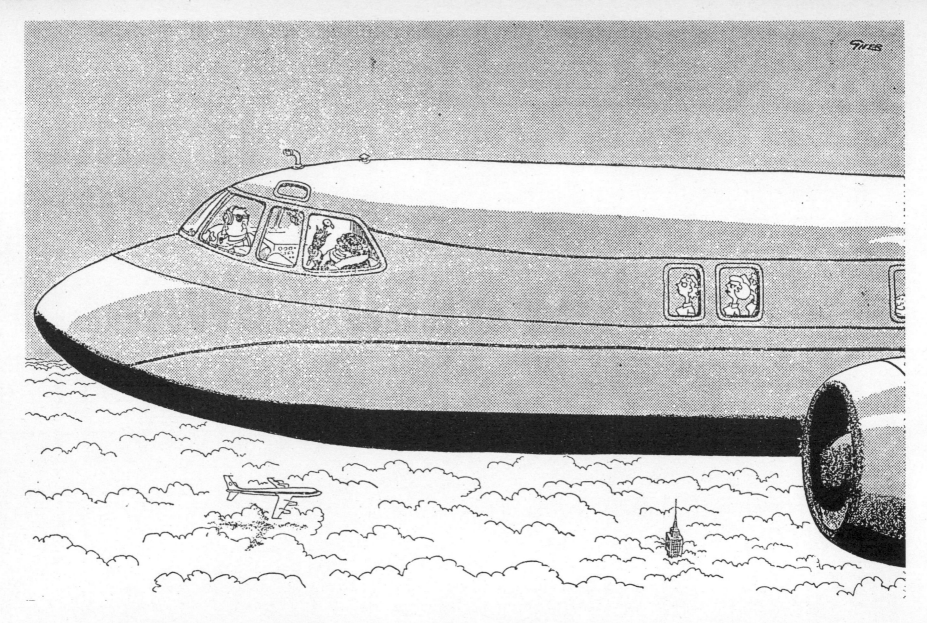

"There won't be any pretty little air hostesses sitting on your lap this trip, my lad."

anothEer anNOuNCemenT of graVe conceRN— GILES family to leave Britain

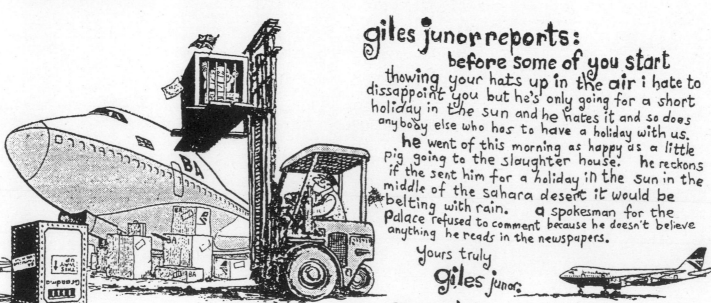

giles junor reports:

before some of you start thowing your hats up in the air i hate to dissappoint you but he's only going for a short holiday in the sun and he hates it and so does anybody else who has to have a holiday with us.

he went of this morning as happy as a little pig going to the slaughter house. he reckons if the sent him for a holiday in the sun in the middle of the sahara desert it would be belting with rain. a spokesman for the palace refused to comment because he doesn't believe anything he reads in the newspapers.

yours truly

giles junor.

P.S. mr wilson has agreed to hang on till we get back and sugarplum thatcher has promised not to declare war on russia for a fortnight.

"Where are you two off to - Moscow, Spain or Wimbledon?"
(Moscow Olympic Games turned into Military Parade by Russians. Holiday makers are well prepared)

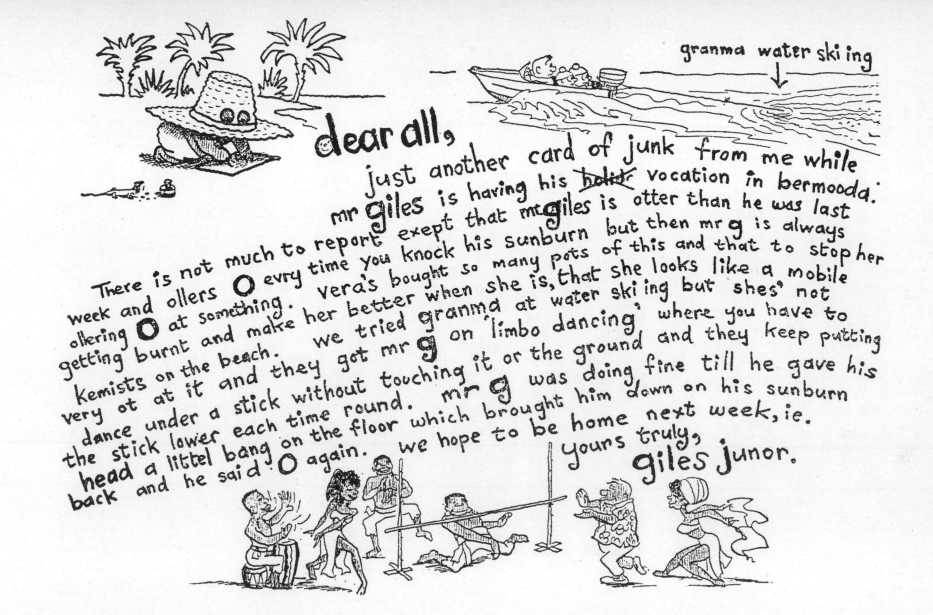

granma water ski ing

dear all,

just another card of junk from me while
mr giles is having his ~~holid~~ vocation in bermooda.
There is not much to report exept that mr giles is otter than he was last
week and ollers O evry time you knock his sunburn but then mr g is always
ollering O at something. vera's bought so many pots of this and that to stop her
getting burnt and make her better when she is, that she looks like a mobile
kemists on the beach. we tried granma at water ski ing but shes' not
very ot at it and they got mr g on 'limbo dancing' where you have to
dance under a stick without touching it or the ground and they keep putting
the stick lower each time round. mr g was doing fine till he gave his
head a littel bang on the floor which brought him down on his sunburn
back and he said O again. we hope to be home next week, ie.

yours truly,
giles junor.

Social

"The one's who haven't won £250,000 on the Pools this week are a bit niggly, aren't they?"

"That's fooled you, Ducks - 'Five hats, thirty-two and elevenpence, PAID."

"YOU say hiring Sabrina to lead yourn in ain't creeping round the judges. WE say it is."

"Brrrp - pardon me."

"I simply spread a rumour that our bell ringers were going
to try to beat those Leicester marathon bell ringers."

"Let me educate you, Honey. Kai-shek ain't a little bear that escaped twice this week at the London Zoo and Chi Chi ain't a general with a little island in the Pacific."

"If I win £75,000, I'm hanged if I don't treat him to a new'n."

"I've had dozens of 'em ever since Lady Lewisham said someone was getting her X certificate before her 11-plus. 'Strand Theatre, stage door, please.'"

(A 10 year old, Janina Faye, takes the part of a sex victim. Lady Lewisham tries to ban the play)

"I'm sure Mr. Marples wouldn't like to hear you call me a nasty name like that just because I keep pushing button B instead of button A."

"I fear our pick-of-the-pops up there is not with the news."

"Like I said - give 'em an inch they'll take a yard. Yesterday it was 'Can I try your crash lid on?'"

"Of course, if you will go lending the coach to any Tom, Dick or Harry, dear…"

"Ladies, I doubt if the Save the Wild Life Fund will agree to letting you have a sub to protect you from the Young Liberals next Friday."

"Standing room only - plenty of seats over the road."

"We've been asked to instruct thee on the gentle art of road sweeping, under Police supervision, lad."

"Relax, madam - EVERYONE has been frisked. Even Sir Robert Mark has been frisked."

"We've got a delegation of hijackers demanding protection from surprise Israeli commando attacks."

"She hasn't been reading the new university report on human gestures.
That one gives us a Harvey Smith every time she passes the camera."

"We think father's costume denotes the spirit of New Year Optimism,
and certainly does not make him look 'a bit of a four letter word' as you put it."

"Finishing off Viscount Linley's bottle was not what head master meant by 'Normal way,' Cholmondeley."

"I thought it wouldn't take them long to get round to that one."

"We'll never fool him - you look as much like a bloody Gillie as I do."

"I fear we must blame that bank manager who let a pretty girl have 14-and-a-half grand without security."

"If we sneaked all our customer's private desires and passions to the Press what do you think they'd make?"

"That wasn't funny, Selina - we allocate those sort of jokes to the other channel."

"This new Geldof gear - I'm having trouble with the 'at."

"He knocked my glass over and there's nothing on there that says I've got to be nice today."

"It's not Elton John nor Robert Maxwell!"

Health

"Whoever said 'These Protest Marches spread like measles' said something."

"Morning, Doctor."

"Coming in here at 87 with nothing worse than a busted bone hits that on the head for a start."

(Winston Churchill operation is a success)

"The committee has passed your wife with flying colours but has grave reservations about you."

"A little bird whispered to me that you wrote to the Prime Minister, telling her we always keep you waiting and she ought to cut our salaries by half."

"Pity, she's escaped out of the back - I was going to let her have a go at humping you up and down to the bathroom."

Sport

"You'd have thought with everyone wearing top hats they wouldn't have missed two of 'em."

The night the Taverners' tavern fell down...Giles was there...

(The British Racing Drivers Club and the Lord Tavener Go-Kart Race at Brands Hatch: Marquee falls down in storm)

ON THE RAILS AT ASCOT .... with GILES

"Yippee, Dad! Here comes ours."

"Thanks to our Russian woman astronaut - she's put a stop to my husband's tired little jokes about women drivers."

"SH!"

"Cheating blighter's! They've switched on a sail!"

"Our Grandma will be the first Grandma to cross the Atlantic in a top hat."

"He couldn't have had much luck with football or the National yesterday - reckons his team ought to be conscripted to build a housing estate on the Aintree course."

"If you checked everything before we left what's Mr. Roy Jenkins doing in the boot?"

(Tories, not happy with the government's policy, decide to get rid of Roy Jenkins)

"They call themselves the Aintree Junior Schools Muggers - cheapest protection for a national runner I've ever had."

"Banning hooligan players has sure put the wind up some of them."

"While you're here, our Women's Lib team could do with a sort-out."

"As a security guard, Corporal Joffre, aren't we giving our services beyond the normal call of duty?"

"Rachel Heyhoe Flint for Captain - that'll make 'em grovel!"

"If there's one fing we've got to stamp out, it's police 'ooliganism."

"You will miss your football hooliganism, Mr Revie - this is Ali, our supporters club secretary."

"Lassie, have you got any other music besides 'Don't cry for me Argentina'?"

"A plague on American Wonder Kid jockey's!"
(Steve Cauthen arrives in the UK)

"On your mark! This is the best chance we've had of winning a Gold yet."
(The Olympic Organisers lost patience with teams threatening to boycott the games. ' If your'e going get out now'.)

"Knock it off Sylvia! The Admiral isn't wearing a funny nose."

"I preferred BA fares when they were sky-high - before I could afford to bring the wife."

"Like we said - we're only here for the sport."

"Whose bright idea was it to come to Iran to protest against British Rail banning booze?"

"You won't beat Borg by paying attention to English fashion notes, Mr McEnroe."

"Me and the boys don't feel this is quite the moment to flog the MCC a W.G. Grace by Leonardo da Vinci."

"I can't see any of our cricketers leaping through the crowd to cuddle their daddies!"

Crime and Punishment

"Delegation to the Governor - that break-in put the wind up 'em."

"We have reason to believe you may be able to assist us in our inquiries."

"These things are sent to try us, as they say."

"A request from next door: Will you kindly stop making that flicking row while he is doing his prep?"

ullo, ullo, ullo,—

hoo dunnit?

giles junor sends in a subjoodicy report on all this 'ere nicking going on inside and outside the nick.

elementry, my dear all,

"It's an odd place for something to be stolen" said a policeman about a painting that was pinched from Scotland yard yesterday, "especially as only police and staff were admitted to the exhibition."

ho, ho, ho, it's just the place i expect anything to get stolen" said mr giles who is still niggly because he had a painting did for the R.N. Lifeboatmen stolen from his exhibition at the earls court boat show this year. he reckons some of their mates disguised as the policemen hopped off with it. enquiries some of their mates disguised as the 'tecs with their i got one of my thik ears off mr g for putting Sir Max aitken and Sir bobby Mark on the short list for today's wage snatch at the daily express and grandma says she bets he wont be making funny jokes like that when they pay his salary with a little goldfish in a jam jar and green stamps. well i must close now and if any of you come across a coloured cartoon of a lifeboat stuck in the mud for Christmas and father Christmas rowing out with their dinner you can phone me at 01-353 8000 or 01-230 1212 (advert) and call for your rewards. or if you run across a purse with £175,000 in it.

yours truly,
giles junor

my thumb

P.S. mr g has so many coppers for mates we call he pierre laval.

"I saw half a dozen screws helping one of 'em with his luggage when he left Norwich."

Military

"Who told B squadron we're doing a fly-over at the Palace when the new baby arrives?"

"They've done one thing the Kaiser and Hitler couldn't do - taken wee Mac's favourite seat."

(German government pays rent for training camps in Scotland)

"Fast as I tell him to 'See 'em off' they tell him to 'Sit'."

"For one who's fiddled his way through every barracks in the kingdom for the past twenty years he's got a nerve."

"Should be an interesting trip, Skipper, assuming you can get her up off the runway."

"Not recognising the Lieutenant in disguise is no excuse -
you are charged with failing to salute a senior officer."

(Plain clothed navel raiding party hijacked HMS Keren: Merchant seamen were in dispute over pay)

Political

"Blimey! Those Cypriots have got him..."
(Archbishop Makarios arrested and deported from Cyprus by British)

"There's going to be some protest marches about 'bull' around here before long."

"All the others want now is an Old Etonian brewer who can play like Stan Matthews, cook like Philip Harben, stand on his head and sing like Elvis Presley."

"We'll have to lower their entrance price out of our tax relief - we're getting more 'Boos' than the ref...."

"Pity, I was just getting the hang of American Rock 'n' Roll."
(America leases airbase to Russians in Kasmir)

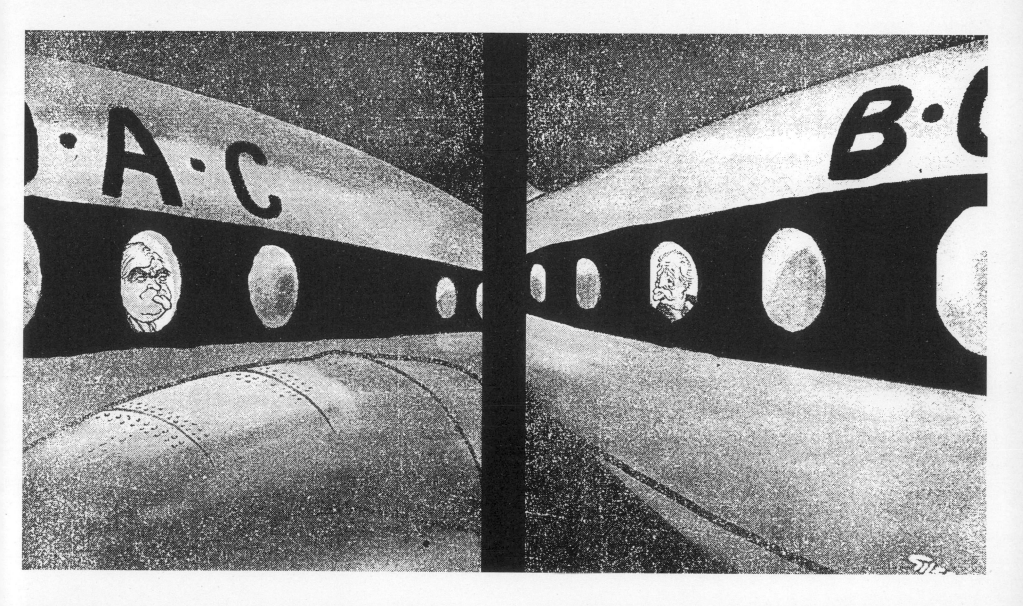

"Mr. Bevan flying to America last night, expected to pass Mr. Macmillan over mid-Atlantic."

"Mr. Macmillan, returning to England last night, expected to pass Mr. Bevan over mid-Atlantic."

"Ma'am, to my knowledge we ain't sent a dog up in ours, but
if we ever do may I be to hell and gone from these islands."

"It is not yet confirmed that H.M Inspectors of Taxes, hearing rumours that O.H.M.S envelopes are being used to carry illegal literature, are making sure their Final Notices get read by despatching them in Christmas Greetings envelopes."

"What's the betting that - who told us this was a quick cut to Scarborough was a Socialist?"

"I'm not pinching it, luv - just putting it in cold storage for a week."

"Here we are, gentlemen - just about as 'average' as the 'average' family with an unemployed husband with fifteen children in four rooms without gas or electricity which that councillor showed you yesterday."

"Never thought I should see the day when I had to book you for poaching, your Lordship."

"Honey, warn Junior not to say 'Gee!' one more time."

"Nice work, lads - ninety-four demonstrators, one King, H.R.H., three bus conductors..."

"All right - which one was it?"

"Of course, if we're going to have the Minister of Agriculture offering free beer to farmers every time one of 'em threatens to shoot him..."

"Well, apart from a few items like Rhodesia, a gas crisis, a by-election, and a rail strike threat, I don't think he's doing much this morning."

"I told you that bounder who asked if we'd like a ride and
left us stuck up here looked a bit like Jim Callaghan."

"Told you so - not only a lot of bull but hundred to one they wouldn't come back this way."
(Harold Wilson meets Rhodesian leader, Ian Smith, on HMS Tiger to try and agree to a settlement following Rhodesia's Unilateral Declaration of Independence in 1965.)

"When you've finished your lecture on what they should have done with the Torrey Canyon in the first place, I've got a little problem for you a bit nearer home."

"It's my fault - I got him up early and said 'Get down the bank and get our cheque back before they cash it and don't come back without it'."

"The wee lassie should have known that any irreverent remark
about drinking constitutes a breach of privilege"

(Scottish Nationalist, Mrs. Winifred Ewing was asked to leave the Commons after saying MPs are a bunch of drunken layabouts)

"If this is another joker with 'Can I lend you a shilling for the meter'
you can tell <u>him</u> to shut up and grow up."

"That's what it says, mate – 'Six geisha girls with bath, c/o H.R.H., Trinity College, Cambridge.' "

"Ted, you remember you invited Mao over to Number 10 for peace talks?"

"Henry, American people have enough problems without you reminding them that Edward Kennedy would not have collected so many votes if he'd protested about the poor oppressed Red Indians."

"Mr. Heath wishes to announce that his sudden confinement and sharp rise in temperature has nothing to do with the Portuguese Prime Minister's visit."

"Dear Margaret, I hope you won't take it amiss if I just say, 'Let the better man win today.'"

"I'm afraid she left by the other door Sir."

"First complaint coming in since the link-up general - polluting outer space with empty bourbon and vodka bottles."

"If my name was Quintin Hogg I would've thought twice before I took
the mickey out of someone named Dingle Foot."

"Hush! Hush! Whisper who dares! The M.P.'s baby is having his din-din.
And the sooner he switches to bottle-feed the better."

"Mr. Toyota emphasises that it is by no means a bribe - simply a token of affection and gratitude."

"I see Prime Minister Trudeau's got his man."

"Well, we've heard a lot about my new image..."

"He was just the same in the old Christine Keeler days...a little
bundle of nerves every time a new name cropped up."

"The Prime Minister feels other affairs of State must come before a Parliament debate on:
'To air or not to air our knickers in the canteen oven'."

"You've got it wrong mate - Paisley's not objecting to the Pope riding Harvey Smith's horse at the Dublin Horse Show."

" Know what today is young fellar? September the twenty-ninth -
known in the best farming circles as 'Muck Spreading Day'. "

"Not much for us Margaret, but there are one or two for that damn boy of ours."

"I don't think Garcon thought much of your 'Good old Maggie! Sock it to 'em Maggie!'"

"No Home Secretary's going to like you not recognising that he's the Home Secretary."

"Prime Minister's orders, m'lord - 'Frisk Willie'."
(Lord Whitelaw peppers two fellow sportsmen after tripping on rough ground whilst on a grouse shoot)

"No, Mr. Heseltine, a U-Boat Captain apologising for sinking one of our ships is one thing, me going to say sorry for the Belgrano is another."

"Very well - I'll see the TUC before I leave if Mr. Scargill doesn't mind me wearing my No.1 Reagan Fan Outfit."

" I think I don't mind you getting married before you leave school,
but I'm not sure how daddy will get along with your groom."

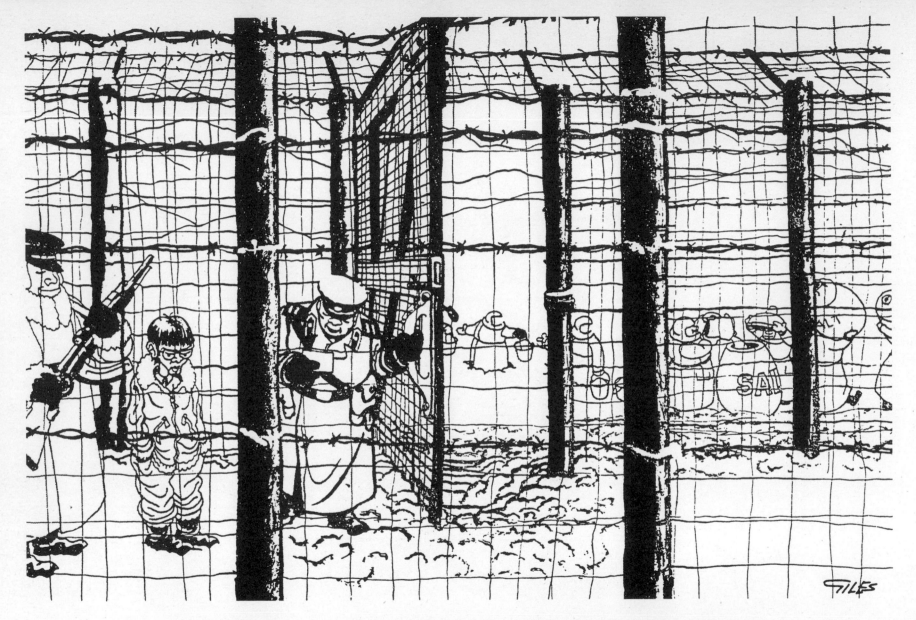

"Only four years? You're a lucky boy - Hess flew a solo stunt out of Germany and got life."

(19 year old Mathius Rust gets four years for landing his plane in Moscow's Red Square)

"Never mind about Tebbit not wanting my 'lousy job'- anyone ever stop to think that I may not be so keen, either."

"Now be a good boy, find a little Brighton Belle, come back and write a book, get it banned and maybe I'll get my diamond brooch."